Copyright © 2018 by Agnesia Agrella. All rights reserved. No part of this publication or the information in it may be quoted from or reproduced in any form by means such as printing, scanning, photocopying or otherwise without prior written permission of the copyright holder.

Thank you to my brother who always protects me.
Thank you for loving me.
For inspiring me to change direction in my life.

You are the reason for this book.

Introduction

Mind your business or Mind your own business is a common English saying that asks for respect of privacy.
It can mean that you are asking other people to stay out of your life or other people can ask you to stay out of their life.
How you manage your life is how you will manage your money. Your life is based on the strategies your body created to survive, from inception to today. Your body's function is to protect you and make sure you survive any perceived or real danger. We, therefore, create co-dependency relationships with the people who take care of us from inception. These strategies become habits, and our body will hardwire pathways in our brain to execute these habits as effectively as possible.
How we then manage our relationships with others will play itself out in how we manage our money.
Whether you allow others to manage your money or you manage other people's money, your body is still executing your survival strategies as effectively as possible.
These co-dependency relationships can create interesting interaction for couples, families, friends, and even business partners. These survival strategies are subconscious

and, most of the time, we are not even aware we are doing it. It is imperative to note that there is nothing wrong with these strategies. The question is: Are your strategies working for you? Are you in control of your life or are other people controlling your life?

If you are asking, *"Why is this always happening to me?" "How could they do that to me?"*

It means an event happened that broke your trust in somebody else.

The question you should be asking is, *"Why am I not minding my own business?"*

I certainly believe it is healthy and everybody's responsibility to mind their own business, meaning their money. Their life is their business, and if treated like a business a lot more people will be financially free.

Mind your own business tip:

Take charge of your finances. If you need support on how to do this, visit:

www.talkmywealth.com

1

"More people should learn to tell their dollars where to go instead of asking them where they went."
Robert Babson

"Hello, it is John, just phoning to see if I can pick up the jet ski this afternoon. I am going to be in the area, and it will make things easy for me."
Hi, as I said when we met, I can only release the Jet ski when the money has cleared into my account," replies Maria.
"I understand; it is just that I am in the area and it will make things so much easier for me."
"John, let me check if the money has been cleared into my account and I will come back to you."
"OK, thank you, will you phone me back, please?" Asks John.
"Sure, I will check with the bank and come back to you." Maria puts the phone down.
It is only 2 days since John said he deposited the money into my account. It normally takes longer than that for a check to clear.
"Well, maybe I should check my account."
Maria is having a conversation with herself.

"Why be difficult. If the money is in my account, why wait?"
But when I bought the Jet ski, the guy let me wait the full 4 days. Insisting he needs to wait for the money to clear. Why be difficult like him?
Like Sarah said, "You are so set in your ways; it has to be your way or no way. You make life so difficult for yourself and people around you."
"Was Sarah right, do I always want things my way, am I just being difficult?"
The only way I will know is to check if the money is in my account. If the money is cleared, I can decide.

Maria walks over to her computer and signs into her bank account. She looks at her bank statement. Yes, the money is showing on her account.
She checks her available balance; yes, it shows the money is available.
"You see, sometimes cheques clear sooner than the time banks say it will." Maria continues the conversation with herself.
So why wait another 2 days?
It is only 10:00 am now; he wants to pick up the Jet ski this afternoon. I still have time to think about it.
Maria goes into the garden and continues weeding the flower bed she was working on

before the phone rang. Still thinking about the transaction.
"It is only 2 days?
How do I know this is not fraud?
Should I wait the full 4 days?
Why be difficult? Am I really difficult and do I want things my way?
I wish Chris was still around; I could have asked him. Is that why we broke up? Do I really just want things my way? No, he left for somebody else. Why should I take him back? How is that being difficult?
Maria, that has nothing to with the Jet ski. What will any reasonable person do?
Maria walks into the kitchen and switches the kettle on for a cup of tea. Hoping that will take her mind off Chris, the break-up and the decision whether she should give in to the pressure from the buyer of her Jet ski to release it today. Or should she wait another 2 days?

Maybe Sarah is right, perhaps I am just being difficult, but then I did not ask for her advice? I thought we were meeting for coffee and catch up to forget about life, not a lecture on how I should conduct my life. I wish she will mind her own business.
You know what; next time, I will tell her:

"Hey, I found your nose; it is in my business again"

Or maybe I will say to her;

"Oh, Sarah, I 'm sorry. I did not realize you are an expert on my life. Please continue while I take notes."

Maria, it is time to *"Keep calm and mind your own business."*

Maria picks up her cup and walks into the garden.

Just like Maria in this story, we all have people in our lives that tell us what to do, even when we do not ask their advice. We all have these conversations with ourselves, which we sometimes cannot stop, and we all have times when we doubt our decisions.

Are you comfortable managing money or do you rather let other people manage your money or do you manage money on behalf of other people?

Do you allow others to manage your money and then wonder why they always tell you what to do?

Do you manage other people's money and then wonder why you should always look after them?

There is a direct relationship between how you manage money and how you are in a relationship with other people. So how does money affect your relationships?

It is not money that affects your relationships; it is the energy around money that affects your relationships. So then how do we create this energy around money and our relationships?

Our bodies create them. I call that strategies to survive. Our bodies' objective is to protect us, and from inception until we die, our bodies will protect us.

Understanding our body and why it thinks an event or situation is dangerous gives us the power to choose and direct our lives rather than being controlled by the events in our lives.

Nothing will bring you greater peace of mind than minding your own business and your money is your business.

Mind your own business tip:

Take a minute to reflect on how well you know your body. Are you an action taker or do you ask somebody to do it for you?

www.talkmywealth.com

2

"Wealth consciousness is so much more than simply having the ability to make money. It is a mindset that involves seeing life, not as a struggle, but as a magical adventure where our needs are met with grace and ease. Wealth consciousness is a state of mind; a sense not of believing, but really knowing that what we need is available to us."
Richard Carlson

It is a month before Christmas; things are slowing down for the end of the year, there is talk that Maria's project will not continue after the holidays.
Lying on her bed thinking about what happened the last 6 months, she broke up with Chris, which means he cancelled the ski holiday with him. She lost the money for for her jet ski, and now she might not have a job after the holidays.
What is the universe trying to tell me? What am I not seeing?
Maria is having another conversation with herself.
"I really like skiing, and I would love to spend Christmas and New Year at a ski resort.
Do I really want to go on my own? Well, why not?

What can I lose? I might meet interesting people. Yes, there will be couples, but I am sure there will be some single people too."
That's it; a decision made. I am going skiing. Maria jumps off her bed, pulls a dress over her head, reaching for her car keys on the dining room table. She shouts to her roommate:
"Maureen, I am going out for a while."
"Where are you going?"
"I am going to the travel agents." I am going skiing in December."
"What, you are doing what?" Do you want to talk about it? Shouts Maureen. You can call the travel agent."
"No, I am not calling them; I am going to see them. See you later." Maria rushes out of the house before Maureen can tell her she is impulsive, why she could not go skiing on her own and why she should think about this.

Two hours later, Maria leaves the travel agent with the booking for a 2-week skiing holiday in St. Johann, Australia, in her hand.
"Wow, that was easy, and I am actually going skiing. On my own. Maria closes the door of her car and takes a deep breath.
O dear, what have I done?
I am going skiing on my own. Well, I will not be the only person in the ski resort, I mean I am not going with a boyfriend or a friend, I

am going alone. Like the travel agent said, there will be activities where I can meet other people in the group, and the tour guides will look after me.

Maria takes the air ticket out of her bag, stare at it for a while, what have I done?

This will be amazing; I have travelled alone before, why will this be any different?

"Well, here I am in St Johann. What a beautiful resort. My room is amazing; now it is just walking into the bar on my own, what will they think, who will I talk to first? Man, why do I do this to myself? Maria, you can do this. I just have to get through the evening. The first night is always the worst. Wow, my heart is racing, why am I so nervous."

"Maria breathes!!!" She says to herself.

Maria takes a deep breath and walks into the bar, "What was I thinking, booking this holiday?"

She walks over to the coat rail. Takes off her coat, hangs it on the coat rail and turns around slowly.

"Look at all these people; they are here with their friends and having a good time." She scans the room, and finally, a couple stops talking.

"Hi," says Linda, would you like to join us? My name is Linda, and this is my husband, Nick.

"Hi, my name is Maria. Please to meet you."

"Can I get you something to drink?" Nick asks.
"Yes please, I will have white wine, Chardonnay please."
Maria feels her body relax and her breathing slowing down. "That was not too bad, and this couple seems nice."
It was an amazing holiday, and the group was perfect. Yes, there were couples, but there were also a group of single friends who lived in different countries and who met up once a year at a ski resort.
Maria loved their stories about how they moved to other countries, how their lives changed.
 "I always wanted to do that. Maybe, just maybe I can do that too."

When Maria got home, she contacted an immigration agent who supported her best friend and his partner to move to the UK 8 months prior.
Three months later, she had her Visa, and she moved to London.
It was when she changed her attitude that her life changed. She could have sat at home thinking and having another conversation with herself about what supposedly went wrong in her life. How she misses Chris and how she should have trusted herself better and not release the Jet ski.

Instead, she decided to have fun, do what she loves, and took action that changed her life. She fulfilled a lifelong dream of moving and working in another county.

Nobody can tell you to make these "Risky" decisions. Only you can make those decisions.

Are you allowing people to talk you out of your dreams or are you taking action to fulfil your dreams?

Sometimes, the Universe has to give us a nudge. I certainly believe the events in Maria's life were the Universe opening doors that she could not see.

We all seek other people's advice because we are always looking for approval and we must live with the decisions we make. But we can direct our lives, or we can let fear direct our lives. It is a choice, and when something is not working for us, we can choose a different way.

Mind your own business tip:

Take a risk doe something that scares. Does not have a big thing like Maria in the story. Start with something small. If you need encouargement contact us at:
https://www.talkmywealth.com/

3

"Success is not to be pursued, it is to be attracted by the person you become."
Richard Carlson

What drives us and what influences our lives is how we manage fear. Fear of what? I hear you ask.

Fear of rejection.

As humans, it takes us much longer than animals to care for ourselves. If we are rejected when we are babies, we will die. Our bodies are programmed to adjust to any situation and in any event to protect us and our caregivers. When our caregivers love us, they will care for us.

Our drive to survive starts at conception and because we cannot survive on our own, we have to create survival strategies.

If the body detects any hint of rejection, it will activate our protection system. We call this our fight, flight, or freeze system.

When our bodies are exposed to the same chemical over a long period of time, we get addicted to our own chemicals.

These behaviours become sub-conscious, and we do not even know we are doing it. The question is, what are you prepared to trade for acceptance?

Are you prepared to allow other people to mind your business so you can be close to them?

Do you mind people's business so that you can be close to them?

What are you really buying?

These might sound like harsh questions, but they are questions to help us understand our own behaviour.

It is the fear of rejection that motivates us to do whatever it takes to survive.

Dr. Joe Dispenza, author of Breaking the habit of being you. Explains:

"We think 60 to 70 000 thoughts per day and 90% of those thoughts are the same as the day before.

Same thoughts always lead to same choices
Same choices lead to the same behaviours
Same behaviours create the same experiences
Same experiences create the same emotions
Same emotions create the same thoughts

Our thoughts create our biology, our neurocircuits, neurochemistry, neurohormones, and even our genetic expression.

How we think, act, and feel is called our personality, and our personality creates our reality.

But if we keep on thinking the same thoughts as the day before, how can we change our lives?

How can we create abundance in our lives when all we know is lack?

According to neuroscience, our brain is organized to reflect everything we know in our life. Our brain is a record of our environment; it is a record or an artefact of our past.

So, if you believe this, then, does your environment control your thinking, or does your thinking control your environment?"

We evolve and change all the time; the question is who do we want to become?

When you change your thinking to think like the person you want to become, you will become that person.

Mind your own business tip:

Learn to create your life.
https://www.talkmywealth.com/

4

"Too many people spend money they haven't earned, to buy things they don't want to impress people they don't know".
Will Rogers

We are bombarded with products and services competing for our pounds and dollars. Everywhere we turn and interact, there are advertisements telling us why we should buy this product or service. With reality TV shows and social media, we are bombarded with celebrity lifestyle and the way they live, and we all want to live in comfort and luxury.

With our need to survive and need for instant gratification and easy access to credit, we have become slaves to our credit cards.

How do we break out of this slavery?

We need to change our environment. When we change our environment, we change our thinking; when we change our thinking, we change our environment.

That is what Maria did when she went skiing. She changed her environment, and she had to get to know other people. The fact that she went skiing on her own, meant there was nobody she could hide behind. She had to speak to other people, people she would never have met if she went with a group or with family and friends. So often, we go in groups to new places, and we never speak to anybody we do not know.

It is not always possible to change our external environment, like Maria in our story. To break our slavery to our own chemicals, we need to change our internal environment, the way we think and the way we behave and our habits. This is not easy, and it is easier if you can change your external environment because that forces your brain to look for new solutions.

When we are constantly looking for acceptance and approval, and we are too scared to change because we are scared the people around us will reject us.

Changing our financial positions and breaking out of fear is a conscious decision. We will play out the above quote until we clear our fear of rejection and when we stop buying other people's approval.

It does not matter whether you work for a boss or for yourself, your money is your business, and if you treat your money as a business, it will work for you!!

A good place to start is to understand your money habits. A Spening Habit Report is a thorough self-examination on how you feel about money. It identifies your limiting beliefs surrounding money and wealth creation. You see a habit is when you are doing something without consciously thinking about. You have done it so many times that your body knows better than you mind how to do it so you don't have to think aobut it anymore. It is now in your subconscious. The only way to change it is to become aware of what you are doing.

This report highlights these hidden convictions, bringing them into conscious awareness.

Recognizing and transforming these beliefs pave the way for a mindset that creates lasting wealth and positive financial behaviours.

How we think affects absolutely everything we do. But did you know that your spending habits do not need to be a mystery?

Spending habits can be accurately measured because they are linked to your thinking preferences!

This insight can bolster your uniqueness, as well as be a starting point for covering any areas where you may be working against yourself.

Mind your own business tip:

You can order your spending habit report at:
www.talkmywealth.com

5

"Live beneath your means – don't make the mistake of looking good and going nowhere."
Robert Kiyosaki

What is money for you? How do you make your money? Do you enjoy the way you make your money?

Living beneath your means is not going to make you rich, but when the money going out is less than the money coming in, you are surviving and are not bankrupt.

What makes you rich is finding ways for your money to work for you rather than you working for money.

That is the secret between the rich and the poor. The rich focus on making money; the poor focus on spending money.

In both cases, they are still buying and spending money; the only difference is the rich buy items that give them more money without them doing anything. E.g., buying real estate that they rent out, writing a book, royalties on music, buying and selling shares, investing in businesses.

It does not matter what you do; there are people who made millions of dollars from it, and there are people who have lost millions of dollars from it.

Then, what is the secret to making millions?

1. It is a choice.

It is a choice to follow your own direction, trust you know best for you and align your thoughts, words, and actions.

2. Enjoy what you do.

Fear and joy are opposite emotions. You can only be in one emotion at a specific time. When you enjoy what you do, your body creates different chemicals. You will have to learn how to walk through your fear, and when you do, you will get addicted to the success chemicals, and success breeds success.

You will then build new connections in your brain. Your body will request more of those chemicals, and you will create situations in your life to produce more of the success chemicals. You will change your addiction from fear of rejection to being addicted to joy.

3. Perseverance

Perseverance is the ability to move forward when things do not go according to plan. Whether you take time to sit and plan or whether you make it up as you go along, you have an expectation of how your life should be and not giving up until you have reached that plan.

4.   Budget for Financial Freedom
Financial freedom is something you work towards. It will not happen without a plan and

Money is the result of your actions, and your actions are a result of your habits and habits are either subconscious or conscious. Subconscious habits are formed through survival strategies.
Conscious habits are acquired through repetition. Repeating the same tasks that will give you the results you want over and over until they become subconscious.

Healthy business habits that create millionaires are acquired just like certain training programmes create Olympic athletes. They chose to be millionaires, they surround them with successful people, they are passionate about their product, they develop and improve their products and service, and they overcome their fear of rejection.
Not everybody wants to be a millionaire, but everybody can be financially free.

Measurement - against your goals and continuous improvement is how you succeed in anything you do. It is key in growing as a person and as a business. The key tasks in measurement are:

- knowing what you want or setting goals
- define your goals in simple wording,
- give your goals a time limit,
- define how you will measure your goals,
- compare your actual performance against your goals,
- evaluate what is working and what is not working
- take corrective action

Measurement and continuous improvement will ensure you achieve your goals.
Success and achievement are just an addiction to other types of chemicals in your body. If you repeat these activities over and over, your body will get addicted to these chemicals.
Ever wondered why some people always seem happy or positive and their lives just fall into place?
They are addicted to the chemicals that produce happy and joyful experiences.
No matter what happened in your life, once you become aware of your habits, you can change them. I am not saying it is easy. I am saying you can change it. Just like an Olympic athlete trains for their medal, millionaires train for their millions. To be

financially free, you must take charge of your finances.
Mind your own business, and your money is your business.

Mind your own business tip:

 Are you ready to take charge of your finances and create the life you want? Make the decision to achieve financial freedom and take action towards it.

www.talkmywealth.com

5

"Cultivate the habit of being grateful for every good thing that comes to you, and to give thanks continuously. And because all things have contributed to your advancement, you should include all things in your gratitude."
Ralph Waldo Emerson

How we bring change into our bodies, is to cultivate the feelings and emotions that we want to feel and who we are deep down. That is Gratitude.

Gratitude is the doorway to cultivating these feelings. When we are so deep in our fight or flight that we go into overwhelm a deep breath and feeling of deep gratitude for something or somebody will change your internal state.

I am not talking when you are in real life or death situation; for example, when you come face to face with a dangerous animal.

This is when we put ourselves into fight or flight through our constant mind chatter. The conversations we have with ourselves about money, what we can and cannot do.

Once we calm down, we can look a situation more objectively, and we can take some time to evaluate the situation from different perspectives. Maybe even get advice from an expert.

When we sit for a while and think about the event where we experienced kindness from somebody or something, you will feel your body relax, you will get a smile on your face, and your heart will slow down, your area in the middle of your chest will warm up, and you will feel your muscles soften. These are the feelings you want to hold onto.

You cannot be in gratitude and fear at the same time. We are naturally kind and loving, and we can practice staying in these feelings. A well thought out "Thank You," instead of a half-hearted "Thanks," often leaves people feeling pretty good. Have you noticed how somebody's face lights up when you look them in the eye and say "thank you" when they have done something kind?

This may sound very simple, but I would like you to put this to the test yourself.

Mind your own business tip:

Over the next week, whenever you feel frustrated, angry, or helpless, take a moment, take a deep breath, and think about an event that you are deeply grateful for. Re-live that experience in all its detail.

www.talkmywealth.com

6

"Intelligent planning is essential for success in any undertaking designed to accumulate riches."
Napoleon Hill

Dreaming small is the biggest reason why most people do not create wealth or the lifestyle they want. Clarity leads to power and clarity of your wealth vision will focus your mind to find a way for you to achieve this vision. Once you are clear on what you want or even if you are clear on what you don't want you can start planning on how to obtain what you want. Nobody know exactly how the futue will unfold but the peple who succeed are the ones who take action. Who are prepared to learn adjust along the way. Just like Maria in our story made a decision to go skiing and then jumped into action. I am suggesting that you do the same. This might sound like a simple story but that is the key to success. Here are the steps to create your financial freedom:

1. Be clear on how much money you want to make in the next year. Be specific on the amount.
2. What are you prepared to give to earn this amount of money? The universe applaud action and when you know

what you are prepared to do to earn that money, you can create a plan. Yes, the plan will change but you can only go in the right direcion when you have a plan.
3. Write down the date by when you want this money.
4. Determine the steps you will take up to the date of when you want to receive this money. It is important to write it down, because then you can compare your progress against your plan weekly. This way you will know what is working and what is not working. Keep what is working, do more of that and stop doing what is not working.
5. Start completing the tasks on your plan.

This is the outline of your plan. Leave space for spontaneity and for new opportunities to come into your life. Have fun with it and be open to be surprised.

Now I want you to become clear on your current financial position. On a piece of paper write down how much money you receive every month. E.g. your salary and other income if you have any.

Then determine how much you spend on the following items:

1. Necessities - Food, electricity, rent, transport to get to work, groceries, money for family.
2. Debt - Loan for your car, loan for your house, credit cards, loans and other debt.
3. Play - Going out and entertainment with friends and family e.g. alcohol, sigaretts
4. Any other expenses not part of the above categories.

I realize that for some your expenses will be more than your income. That is OK. It is more important that you want to change your situaion. I know it is going to be difficult and it will take effort and action. Are you prepared to take the action?

Now I want to introduce you to the Financial Galaxy Map, a new approach to budgetting and managing your money. This is where the hard work will start because in some areas of your life you will be spending to much money and you will have to adjust.

If your expenses are more than your income you will be the first to say *"I cannot do this"*. For you I totally understand. It will take you a bit longer to make the adjutments but you have to start somewhere.

Everybody has to start where they are today. The steps in the plan above will support you to make the changes until you have worked

yourself out of your current situation. Perseverance is key.
Use the Financial Galaxy Map to re-allocate your income to the following categories:
1. Necessity Nexus - 55% (Essentials for survival, like food, housing, and bills)
2. Freedom Orbiter - 10% (Financial Freedom Account, for investments or retirement)
3. Long-Term Savings Station - 10% (Long-Term Savings, for big goals like a house or car)
4. Play Planet - 10% (Play Account, guilt-free spending on fun)
5. Education Explorer - 10% (Education, for personal growth or career advancement)
6. Charity Comet - 5% (Giving back, donations, or supporting causes)

This map is about shifting your thoughts about yourself and your relationship with money. Remember money isn't just numbers on a piece of paper; it's energy. And if you want that energy to flow your way, you've got to be open to it. Think, believe, and get yourself into rooms where money is a natural part of the conversation. Once you shift your mindset to how can I do this, the people who can support you to achieve your financial freedom will enter your life. You don't have to know how right now.

If you are still struggling to find meaning or motivation to implement your Finacial Galaxy map, step back and ask, "How can I serve?" Sometimes, we lose perspective when we're too focused on our problems. But when we shift that focus outward, incredible things start to happen.
Nobody has ever accumulated wealth and riches on their own. All your plans should be a collaboration with other people. Your family, your friends and people who want to see you succeed. Find people who will support you. If your first plan which you adopt does not work, speak to people who are more successful than you and adopt your plan.

Mind your own business tip:

Your are more powerful than you think, start working with the new budget and if you need support, our North Star Planner can support you to implement this budget. It is available on Amazon and you will find more information on our website.
https://www.talkmywealth.com/

www.ingramcontent.com/pod-product-compliance
Lightning Source LLC
Chambersburg PA
CBHW031517210526
45464CB00007B/2949